KidCaps' Presents

The Iraq War
A History Just for Kids

KidCaps is An Imprint of BookCaps™
www.bookcaps.com

Table of Contents

About KidCaps

KidCaps is an imprint of BookCaps™ that is just for kids! Each month BookCaps will be releasing several books in this exciting imprint. Visit are website or like us on Facebook to see more!

Troops in Iraq get ready to fight[1]

Introduction

Freddy Watkins was a private in the United States Marine Corps. Born and raised in Indiana, U.S.A., he knew since he was a kid that he wanted to be a soldier when he grew up. When he played war with his friends, it wasn't a game for him; it was training. All during high school he tried to exercise and eat well so that he could qualify for basic training with the Marines. And the day after graduation, when he turned 18, he went with his parents to the local recruiting center and signed up to join the Marine Corps.

Basic training had been tough, but he had passed, along with most of his team. Shortly after graduation, he and his unit were assigned to Kuwait. No one knew exactly why they were there, but everyone knew that something important was going to happen soon. Troops from around the country were being sent to Kuwait and massed together on the border with Iraq. After the terrorist attacks of September 11th, lots of guys like him had joined the ranks of the military to hunt down the bad guys and to bring them to justice. Whenever Freddy thought about the twin towers falling, and all of those people who died, his blood boiled and he started to tingle all over. A lot of people got sad when they thought about September 11th; but not Freddy, Freddy just got mad.

In March of this year, Freddy and the rest of his unit were told to move north into Iraq. This was the first time that most of the men had experienced real combat, and it was pretty scary. There were planes flying overhead dropping bombs, tanks in front of them clearing the roads, and large trucks that carried him and his fellow soldiers from one village to the next, arresting enemy fighters and sometimes getting into firefights with them.

Now, here he was in Baghdad. The Iraqi government had been overthrown already, and the mission of Freddy and his men was to maintain the security in Iraq's capital city. He was to patrol the borders of the area known as the "Green Zone" and make sure that no Iraqi rebels attacked the new military and governmental headquarters in the country. Freddy shuttered as he thought about some of the ways that Iraqi rebels fought. Because they had older weapons, less money, and smaller numbers than the Americans and British, they used their imaginations to cause all kinds of problems. Sometimes they had snipers shoot at the American soldiers without any warning, sometimes they attacked at night, and sometimes they put bombs inside of cars and drove them right through the checkpoints around the edge of the Green Zone.

But the weapon that had killed some of Freddy's men was something called an IED, an Improvised Explosive Device. IEDs were kind of like homemade bombs that were hard to see. Sometimes they were buried in the sand and sometimes they were hidden under large pieces of garbage on the side of the road. When the soldiers went out of the Green Zone and into the city, they traveled in long lines of trucks and armored cars called "convoys". Every time that they saw something on the side of the road everyone would hold their breath, wondering if it was a bomb. Sometimes cars pulled up next to them, and the passengers started to shoot large guns, and sometimes they heard gunshots but couldn't see where they were coming from.

The result was that Freddy and his men were nervous all the time. Every Iraqi that they saw might be an enemy, every pile of garbage might be a bomb, and every *pop* might be the bullet that kills them. Freddy couldn't sleep at night; he had so many nightmares. He felt like he couldn't trust anyone who wasn't an American, not even the Iraqis that were on his side. He had heard that some soldiers were going home because of the stress and that a few had even committed suicide, and Freddy wondered where he would be in six more months. His unit wasn't scheduled to go home until then.

Together with a group of three soldiers, Freddy held his gun and squinted against the sun. Iraq was under control of the Americans, but it sure didn't feel like the fighting was going to stop anytime soon. That meant that Freddy had a job to do. It wasn't easy, and it might not be popular, but it was his job. Taking a deep breath Freddy gave the order to move out, and he and his men walked along the Green Zone border to keep the people inside safe.

The Iraq War was different from other wars before it. For most of the war, there were no clear battle lines, no clear military goals, and it wasn't always easy to know who your friends were and who your enemies were. The world community wasn't sure whether or not to support the war, and it seemed like the fighting just never stopped. Some people compared it to the Vietnam War, which was a war famous for its violence and for the lack of communication between the two sides.

In this book, we will be taking a closer look at the Iraq War, which was fought from 2003-2011. Almost 4,500 American soldiers died during the war, and another 33,000 were wounded. Over 110,000 Iraqis, both soldiers and civilians, would eventually die in the fighting also. But do you know what led up to the war? In the next chapter, we will see how the Gulf War, fought in 1991, planted the seeds of the Iraq War. Specifically, the war that Saddam Hussein chose to deal with the international community caused serious problems and made other nations want to invade his country.

Then we will see why the war happened. In his speech just before the Iraq War began, President George W. Bush explained the main reasons for the bombing and invasion of Iraq. We will look at each of the reasons one by one, and you can decide for yourself whether or not you agree with them and whether or not you think it was a good idea to invade Iraq.

Then we will see what happened during the war. We will see that the war was divided up into two phases: the initial combat phase and then the rebuilding phase. The rebuilding phase is what took the longest and was the most difficult. The fighting in Iraq seemed to go on and on, and as American soldiers kept dying in the fighting, people back home in the United States started to think that the war was not such a brilliant idea after all. Several stories that came out in the news made some Americans think that the White House was not truly doing a good job in Iraq at all. Also, we will see that the use of private citizens to rebuild Iraq was unpopular with some Americans and even led to some problems.

Then we will see what it was like to be a kid during the Iraq War. Whether you were a kid living in Iraq during the fighting or were back in the United States learning about it in school, you would have been sure to have had an opinion about all the fighting and violence. Also, people that you knew and loved would have been affected by the war, something decided by people in an office far away.

Then we will learn about how the Iraq War ended. After a long time, the rebuilding phase finally came to a close, and the American troops left Iraq. Were they successful in their mission to leave Iraq a better place than they found it? The following chapter will show us what Iraq is like today and how many people view the 2003 Iraq War.

Your parents probably remember the Iraq War quite well, so why not ask them to talk about as you read through this book. That way, you may be able to learn about what their life was like back then and what they thought about the war. Are you ready to learn more? Great! Let's get started.

Chapter 1: What Led Up To the Iraq War?

Most people don't like war; war is expensive, a lot of people get hurt and die, and long friendships with other countries can get ruined practically overnight. Most nations try to use what's called *diplomacy* to avoid fighting. They have ambassadors to represent their leaders, they have representatives go the organizations like the United Nations, where nations can talk out their problems, and they have secret communications to solve small issues before they get bigger. There are also other methods of keeping bad countries from becoming worse: for example, economic sanctions (punishments) make sure that bad countries can't do business with anyone, and so they lose lots of money. Most countries, when they have to experience economic sanctions, decide to stop doing the bad things that made everyone so angry. But sometimes, diplomacy, meetings in the United Nations, economic sanctions, and even secret communications can't stop some bad leader from doing bad things. In those rare situations, sometimes a war has to happen.

For United States President George W. Bush and British Prime Minister Tony Blair, the 2003 Iraq War was just such a situation. But what kinds of things had happened that made them feel that way? Let's find out.

In 1980, Iraq invaded the neighboring nation of Iran and, for eight years, fought a long and bloody war. During that war, the Iraqi president, Saddam Hussein, used awful chemical weapons against the Iranian people, killing many thousands of them. The war ended in 1988, but two years later President Saddam Hussein invaded another neighboring nation, called Kuwait, and took it over. The Kuwaiti people were treated badly by the Iraqi military, and it looked like President Hussein might keep attacking other nations, including Saudi Arabia, who provided oil for much of the world. In the United Nations, it was decided to go to war against Iraq and a large group of countries (called "The Coalition") got together to fight the war. In less than two months, the Coalition had won. Saddam Hussein removed his troops from Kuwait and promised to allow United Nations weapons inspectors into his country to make sure that there were no dangerous chemical, nuclear, or biological weapons. Because they could hurt so many people, both soldiers and innocent civilians, their weapons were called Weapons of Mass Destruction.

After the 1980 war with Iran and the 1991 war against the Coalition (called the Gulf War) many of the people of Iraq thought that it was time to have a new leader in their country. In the North and in the South, groups of Iraqi people tried to rise up against Saddam Hussein and to force him to stop being president. However, instead of listening to what the people of his country wanted, President Hussein killed anyone who tried to stop him. Tens of thousands of people, mostly innocent civilians, were killed by their own president as they expressed their views. The world was shocked to see how Saddam Hussein treated his own people, people of his own country.

Saddam Hussein was a strict leader and didn't allow any rebellion[2]

In the meantime, the United Nations inspectors weren't having an easy time doing their job in Iraq. As we saw earlier, part of the condition of ending the Gulf War was that Saddam would allow U.N. inspectors into his country to make sure that he wasn't making or using any Weapons of Mass Destruction and that any older weapons that he had were being destroyed. But the inspectors didn't

[2] Image source: http://www.biography.com/people/saddam-hussein-9347918

always feel welcome in Iraq, weren't always allowed to go anywhere they wanted, and sometimes they weren't even allowed across the border.

The world saw what was happening in Iraq, and because the Iraqi government (led by Saddam Hussein) wasn't keeping up their end of the bargain they agreed to during the Gulf War and they weren't cooperating fully with the United Nations, the United Stated (under President Bill Clinton) and Great Britain (under Prime Minister Tony Blair) decided to start a four day bombing campaign of key targets in Iraq. Called "Operation Desert Fox", the attacks took place from December 16-19, 1998. Over 600 Iraqi people died in the bombings and Iraq realized how serious the situation was. But, despite the threats and the bombings, Saddam Hussein was not willing to cooperate with the rest of the world and became more angry and stubborn. News reports made it clear that Iraq would no longer allow any United Nations inspectors inside its borders ever again.

Around this time, the Unites States started to receive some pretty worrying reports from their spies. Called "intelligence", these reports made it look like Iraq was still producing Weapons of Mass Destruction and that some of them might even be nuclear. In the news and in front of different governmental meetings, the American people heard about all of the damage that these weapons could do, how many Americans could die, and how dangerous Iraq, and in particular Saddam Hussein, still was.

Secretary of State Colin Powell went before the
United Nations to explain how serious the Weapons
of Mass Destruction in Iraq truly were[3]

Some of the reports made it seem like bombs and
explosions, and American deaths seemed a long ways
off. Problems in the Middle East were so far away
that it seemed almost like watching a movie and not
real life. A lot of Americans heard the scary reports
but didn't actually take them very seriously; that is,
they didn't until September 11, 2001.

Do you remember the terrorist attacks of September
11, 2001? Do you remember where you were and
what you were doing? If you were too little, why not
ask your parents of other adults that you may know
what they remember from that day? On September
11, four planes were stolen from airports on the East
Coast and were used like giant missiles to attack the

---

[3]   Image   source: http://news.xin.msn.com/en/silverlight-gallery.aspx?cp-documentid=5225258&page=15

World Trade Center building, the Pentagon, and a target in Washington D.C. The plane headed towards Washington D.C. never made it because some brave passengers fought against the terrorists, and the plane crash landed in a rural area of Pennsylvania.

The American people, and truly the whole world, were shocked at what happened on September the 11th. Just 19 men, smaller than any army in any country, were able to cause so much damage and pain to so many people. Americans and the White House began to think about terrorism more seriously and to realize that terrorists had to be stopped before they made it to the United States.

The Twin Towers were destroyed on September 11, and thousands of innocent people died[4]

[4] Image source: http://e29backroad.blogspot.com/2012/11/911-first-person-account_16.html

As it tends to happen after a lot of tragedies, there was a lot of confusion and misunderstandings flying around after the attacks of September 11th. One of the news reports that was repeated man times was that Iraq had supported the terrorist group (Al-Qaeda) that had carried out the attack on 9/11. For the White House, hearing that Iraq, whom they already suspected of making and storing Weapons of Mass Destruction, had been somehow connected to the attacks of September 11th was too much. They thought that Iraq had to be stopped and that it was causing too much trouble to too many people.

The United Nations agreed that something had to be done and that the economic sanctions that they had been using didn't seem to be working. So, the U.N. Security Council sent out Resolution 1441 on November 8, 2002. The resolution gave Iraq one more chance to live up to the terms of its surrender from 1991, to stop buying and making dangerous weapons, and to pay to Kuwait the money they owed them from the Gulf War attacks. The representatives who wrote the resolution were careful not to make it look like war would automatically follow if Saddam didn't obey. In fact, Saddam did agree to let the U.N. inspectors back in after the resolution was passed. However, the United States didn't think that he was serious but that he was playing political games to buy a little bit of time.

By early 2003, the United States was getting impatient. Even though some people thought that Iraq was doing more to cooperate with the United Nations orders, others didn't think that they were doing enough and that they were hiding something. President Bush insisted that Iraq was still violating the terms of the Resolution and that the Security Council should meet together again to decide what to do. France promised not to support any action leading to war, and the United States and the United Kingdom insisted that war was the only way to stop Saddam Hussein and his dangerous government. A deadline was set by the U.S. and the U.K. on March 17, 2003, to cooperate 100% with the U.N. standards. They gave Iraq just 48 hours to act.

The United Nations wanted to give Iraq more time, but the U.S. and U.K. didn't want to wait. Without the permission of their fellow leaders, these two nations started to build up large numbers of troops in Kuwait to prepare for bombing and an invasion of Iraq. On March 20, 2003, after the 48 hour deadline had come and gone, a massive bombing campaign, called a "Shock and Awe" campaign, was launched in order to weaken main Iraqi targets. At the same time, the soldiers in Kuwait invaded from the south and Iraqis trained by the CIA in the North began to move towards the capital city of Baghdad. The fighting started quickly at about 5:30 in the morning and got serious quickly.

The Iraq War had officially begun.

Chapter 2: Why Did the Iraq War Happen?

As we saw earlier, no one actually ever wants a war. But sometimes, when all the other options have been tried, a war can't be avoided. For U.S. President Bush and U.K. Prime Minister Blair, they had tried all of the peaceful solutions but Iraq was still too dangerous to be left alone. On March 20, 2003, these two men started the Iraq War. But what were their main reasons for doing so? Although they were many reasons given to the American public and given to the world community, a speech that President Bush gave on March 19 (the day before the bombing and invasion started) lays out his reasons for thinking that the Iraq War was a good idea.

---

[5] Image source: http://www.youtube.com/watch?v=8OCvq-x6pZ0

President Bush talked about the invasion of Iraq on March 19, 2003[5]

Let's see what President Bush said in that important speech.

> "My fellow citizens, at this hour, American and coalition forces are in the early stages of military operations to disarm Iraq, to free its people and to defend the world from grave danger…To all the men and women of the United States Armed Forces now in the Middle East, the peace of a troubled world and the hopes of an oppressed people now depend on you…I want Americans and all the world to know that coalition forces will make every effort to spare innocent civilians from harm. A campaign on the harsh terrain of a nation as large as California could be longer and more difficult than some predict. And helping Iraqis achieve a united, stable and free country will require our sustained commitment.

We come to Iraq with respect for its citizens, for their illustrious civilization and for the religious faiths they practice. We have no ambition in Iraq, except to remove a threat and restore control of that country to its own people...Our nation enters this conflict reluctantly -- yet, our purpose is sure. The people of the United States and our friends and allies will not live at the mercy of an outlaw regime that threatens the peace with weapons of mass murder. We will meet that threat now, with our Army, Air Force, Navy, Coast Guard and Marines, so that we do not have to meet it later with armies of fire fighters and police and doctors on the streets of our cities...My fellow citizens, the dangers to our country and the world will be overcome. We will pass through this time of peril and carry on the work of peace. We will defend our freedom. We will bring freedom to others and we will prevail."[6]

This speech was important because it was the first that many Americans had heard about the invasion of Iraq. President Bush wanted everyone to understand why the government had decided to send troops to fight in Iraq and why they should support the war effort. Did you see the reasons that were given to the American public? Do you see the clear connection

---

[6]   Quotation   source:
http://edition.cnn.com/2003/US/03/19/sprj.irq.int.bush.transcript/

with the terrorist attacks of September 11th? Let's highlight a few of the most important sentences.

- **"American and coalition forces are in the early stages of military operations to disarm Iraq, to free its people and to defend the world from grave danger."** This sentence clearly explains what the United States and United Kingdom wanted to achieve by invading Iraq. They wanted to take care of the whole Weapons of Mass Destruction (WMD) problem. They wanted the replace Saddam Hussein as president, because he was such a cruel person. And they wanted to stop Iraq from supporting terrorist groups like Al-Qaeda.

Those three goals were the whole reason that the Iraq War was fought. Do they sound like good reasons to you? They sounded pretty good to most Americans back in 2003. But does it surprise you that France and many other nations did not support the Iraq War? If there were such solid reasons to invade Iraq, why didn't everyone get involved, like they had in previous wars? We will learn later that of the three reasons used to invade Iraq, two of them weren't actually true at all! Some nations were worried that might be the case and wanted to investigate more, but the United States and Great Britain were worried that waiting longer might mean more deaths and so were eager to get Saddam Hussein and his government out of power.

However, did you note another fascinating quote from the speech? Check it out below:

- **"The people of the United States and our friends and allies will not live at the mercy of an outlaw regime that threatens the peace with weapons of mass murder. We will meet that threat now, with our Army, Air Force, Navy, Coast Guard and Marines, so that we do not have to meet it later with armies of fire fighters and police and doctors on the streets of our cities."** What do you think President Bush was talking about when he mentioned fire fighters, police, and doctors fighting a war on the streets of our cities? There can be no doubt: President Bush was talking about the attacks of September 11th. Right or wrong, he felt that invading Iraq would stop future terrorist attacks in the Unites States.

Some people accused President Bush of using peoples' emotions and fear to gain support for the war, and maybe they are right. Either way, many Americans thought, and continue to think, that the invasion of Iraq was directly related to the attacks of 9/11. Do you agree with them? Do you think it was right to connect the two events?

In other speeches and conferences, President Bush also made it clear that he wanted to invade Iraq because of its human rights violations. Do you know what human rights are? The phrase "human rights" refers to the things that anybody should be allowed to do, like have a job, live peacefully, and not be afraid of the government. In Iraq, anyone who disagreed with the government quickly found themselves in a lot of trouble so it could be said that Saddam was violating the human rights of his citizens. Like we saw in the above speech, President Bush wanted to free the people of Iraq and give them back their country. Instead of living under a tyrant (a bad leader) he wanted to let them be a government like the United States, where people can choose their own presidents and make their own laws.

As you can see, the Iraq War happened to protect both the Iraqi people from a dangerous leader and Americans from his weapons and from any future terrorist attacks. While some of the reasons ended up being wrong, at the time the war was supported by a large group of Americans and British citizens, although other countries thought that it was a bad idea.

Chapter 3: What Happened During the Iraq War?

The Iraq War received a special mission name: Operation Iraqi Freedom. The name of the mission was to remind everyone what the American and British militaries were fighting for. They were fighting together with the Iraqi people to get rid of a tyrannical leader and a bad government. That was the idea.

Operation Iraqi Freedom started with smart bombs being launched against important building in the capital city of Baghdad. Most people who were watching the war from far away thought that the war would be similar to the 1991 Gulf War, where a long period of bombing was followed by a short invasion. Imagine their surprise when they learned that American and British soldiers invaded Iraq right after the bombing started. The huge number of bombs falling from the sky and the large amount of soldiers (over 200,000 troops) invading from the south were meant to scare the Iraqis into not fighting. And it seems like the tactic worked.

The Iraqi military surprised the Coalition troops by not using a "scorched earth" policy. Have you ever heard of a scorched earth policy before? It is where one army destroys everything as they run away so that the other side cannot use it to get stronger. Sometimes, this means destroying bridges, roads, houses, crops, and even killing animals so that they can't be eaten. During the 1991 Gulf War, the Iraqi troops set fire to more than 600 oil wells as they left Kuwait and caused a lot of problems for the other side. Everyone thought that the Iraqi would do the same thing in 2003, but most of them just surrendered, and the Coalition troops were able to move forward quickly. By March 25, they were only 60 miles outside of Baghdad.

An enormous dust storm made everyone slow down a little bit and so there was a bit of a pause in the fighting.

A soldier took a picture of a 2003 dust storm in Iraq. Can you see why everyone had to stop fighting?[7]

But the pause didn't last too long. Within a short time, the guns were making noise again and the Coalition troops kept pushing forward towards the capital city. On April 4, the Baghdad airport was captured, and on April 9 the entire city was under American control. That same day, a major city named Basra in the south of the country was captured by British forces. The government and leaders of Iraq had since run away, and no one knew where they were.

On April 13, 2003, there was a real victory when Saddam Hussein's hometown of Tikrit was captured by American forces. Although several smaller areas had to be brought under control and borders had to be set up and protected, it looked like Operation Iraqi Freedom was going to be a success. In fact, on May 1, President Bush visited the *USS Abraham Lincoln*, an aircraft carrier that had just returned from battle in the Persian Gulf area. After making an impressive landing aboard an airplane, he gave an exciting speech with a large banner behind him that said "Mission Accomplished".

22ImageId%22%3A24478812%7D

President Bush during his "Mission Accomplished" speech[8]

Why did the banner say "Mission Accomplished" if there was still fighting going on? The speech given by President Bush was meant to show that Iraq was now under control of the Coalition but that there was still some rebuilding work to do and that Saddam Hussein still had to be found. However, many people were upset when they saw the banner. Have a look at a few excerpts from the speech to see if you can find out why:

> "My fellow Americans, major combat operations in Iraq have ended. In the battle of Iraq, the United States and our allies have

[8] Image source: http://en.wikipedia.org/wiki/File:Bush_mission_accomplished.jpg

prevailed. And now our coalition is engaged in securing and reconstructing that country...We have difficult work to do in Iraq. We're bringing order to parts of that country that remain dangerous. We're pursuing and finding leaders of the old regime who will be held to account for their crimes. We've begun the search for hidden chemical and biological weapons, and already know of hundreds of sites that will be investigated. We are helping to rebuild Iraq where the dictator built palaces for himself instead of hospitals and schools...The transition from dictatorship to democracy will take time, but it is worth every effort. Our coalition will stay until our work is done and then we will leave and we will leave behind a free Iraq."[9]

Can you understand why some people got upset when they saw the banner and heard the speech? Some people thought that President Bush was saying that the dangerous part of the war was over and that everyone should celebrate. Of course, in his speech the President made it clear that there would still be work to do, but it seems like no one knew just how dangerous Iraq actually was. At the time the speech was given, 141 Americans had been killed in the fighting. But before the war would finally end in 2011 (eight years later) 4,347 more would be killed. In other words, almost 97% of the soldiers killed in Iraq

[9]   Quotation   source: http://articles.cnn.com/2003-05-01/us/bush.transcript_1_general-franks-major-combat-allies?_s=PM:US

would die after the President had said "Mission Accomplished".

The challenge after taking over the city, as the President had said, would be to rebuild Iraq. Schools, hospitals, and governmental offices had to be built, and local Iraqis had to be trained as politicians, policemen, and as soldiers. The idea was to teach the Iraqis how to take care of their own country, without Saddam Hussein bossing them around. But after the bad leaders and the bad government disappeared, something unexpected happened: the Iraqi people couldn't decide who they wanted to be their leader and they started a civil war. One side wanted the Americans to help, and the other side wanted the Americans to leave Iraq right away. The ones who wanted the Americans to leave and who were unhappy with the new Iraqi government being put together were called "insurgents", or rebels.

The insurgents were fewer in number and didn't have the same weapons or money to fight as the Coalition troops did. So instead of fighting a traditional war, the insurgents would use car bombs, traps, and snipers to attack American and British troops before running away. Some insurgents would even hide bombs under their clothing, walk to a crowded marketplace or military checkpoint, and then detonate the bomb to kill themselves and everyone around them. Lots of soldiers were wounded and killed this way. Those who survived often went home missing and arm or a leg. The fighting was dangerous and scary.

There was a bright spot during all of the tense fighting when Saddam Hussein was discovered hiding in a small hole on December 13, 2003. The hole was dug on a farmhouse hear his hometown of Tikrit. Saddam had some money with him, but it was clear that he had been hiding for a long time. He looked different than he had when he was in power.

This picture of Saddam Hussein was taken moments after he was pulled out of his hiding place[10]

There was a trial in an Iraqi court, and on December 30, 2006, he was executed by his own people for all the bad things he had done and crimes he had committed during his time as president. But although Saddam had been executed, the fighting went on in Iraq.

---

[10] Image source: http://en.wikipedia.org/wiki/File:SaddamSpiderHole.jpg

Because things didn't look like they were getting any better, during January and February of 2007, President Bush decided to send 20,000 more troops to Iraq, mainly to the city of Baghdad, to get the situation under control. After surviving many more attacks by insurgents, which seemed to kill Americans almost every day, new U.S. President Barack Obama announced a "drawdown" of troops in Iraq that would begin in 2010. By August, all but 50,000 troops had left, and the mission was no longer about fighting, but more about maintaining stability in the country. The Coalition wanted to Iraqis to fight their own civil war and to solve their own problems, and the Americans would only be there to help a little while longer before leaving.

The Iraq War lasted over eight years from start to finish. At first, many Americans agreed that U.S. soldiers should go and fight in that war. However, as time went by, their opinions started to change. What kind of things influenced their opinions?

One key factor was the news. News reports of the terrible fighting and slow progress made some people think that all of those American soldiers were dying for nothing. Other news reports talked about how Americans were mistreating Iraqi prisoners, and it made the situation look like it was getting out of control. Also, some 100,000 "Private Military Contractors" were hired by the United States to go to Iraq and work in different areas. Some worked in construction, some worked in security, and some actually participated in the fighting. But as reports surfaced of these contractors becoming violent with Iraqi citizens, more and more Americans decided that they thought that the Iraq War had been a lousy idea, or at the very best that it had not been handled well by the White House.

The Iraq War was becoming unpopular with everyone involved, even the politicians and the soldiers.

Chapter 4: What Was It Like To Be a Kid During the Iraq War?

A child sits on tops of a ruined building in Iraq[11]

Have you ever heard the sound of a gunshot or seen fireworks light up the sky? Depending on the circumstances, those things can be cool and exciting. But imagine those same types of explosions in your neighborhood, destroying houses and killing people you know and love. Seems a lot scarier, right?

---

[11] Image source: http://thesituationist.wordpress.com/2007/06/28/our-soldiers-their-children-the-lasting-impact-of-the-war-in-iraq/

In Iraq, kids saw the world around them crumble and fall apart. Their president, their community, their schools, their friends…everything changed almost overnight. It wasn't strange to see dead bodies (both Iraqi and American) in the streets or to have to listen to people crying over family members that had been killed.

As a kid, sometimes war is hard to understand. You wonder why everyone can't just stop fighting and talk about their problems, like you do with your friends at school. You can't understand why anyone would use bombs and guns to get their way. At school, they tell us that fighting is bad, so it's strange to see grown-ups doing what kids aren't allowed to. During the Iraq War, lots of kids had to listen to the bombs and wonder if the next one was going to fall on their house. They were scared to go to the store because of the insurgents and their bombs, so it seemed like there was no safe place to go. Can you imagine being scared all the time? What do you think life will be like for those kids when they grow up?

Even though the war has since ended, you can imagine how some of those kids still have distressing dreams and feel sad about everything that happened.

In the United States kids saw the Iraq War on TV and then later saw the veterans coming home with injuries and sad looks on their faces. Even though they were never worried about dying in a war, do you think that American kids got sad when they thought about it too?

American kids could have talked to their parents to try and understand what was happening. They could have asked why the war was happening and what it all meant. Even though their parents might not have all the answers, kids would at least get to think a little about what was happening and why. And when they saw the news reports about how awful things were over there and how many people were dying, you can be sure that some kids got pretty sad.

War is hard on everybody, but kids are the ones who can't really run away or do anything about it. In other words, it's no good to be a kid during a war.

Chapter 5: How Did the Iraq War End?

For years, the fighting had been fierce in Iraq. During regular patrols soldiers would be ambushed by insurgents or would worry about running over a bomb and dying or being captured. Then suddenly, President Obama announced a troop drawdown and by August 2010 there were only 50,000 soldiers left who would work primarily as trainers and peacekeepers. Then, on December 15, 2011, a small ceremony was held in Baghdad and the last fighting soldiers left Iraq (although a few thousand stayed behind on permanent bases).

From such a tremendous start to such a quiet finish, the Iraq War surprised people at every turn. Some people were expecting momentous speeches or fireworks, but it all ended when the U.S. government realized that the civil war in Iraq was not going to be solved with American guns. After having made sure that there were no more Weapons of Mass Destruction in Iraq, that Saddam Hussein was no longer in power, and that the Iraqi people were free to decided how they wanted their country to be run, President Obama decided that the time had come to bring the troops home.

When the soldier left Iraq, they left a country that still had a weak economy, still had some fighting between the religious and political groups, and still had some serious problems.

What happened after the Iraq War?

After the Iraq War ended, the soldiers all went home to the United States and Britain. Some of them began to have serious emotional problems because of all of the stress that they had while in Iraq. Do you remember what it was like day to day in Iraq? The American soldiers never knew when they would be attacked, and sometimes they didn't even know who their friends were and who their enemies were. When they came home, it was hard for some of the soldiers to get used to peacetime. Sometimes they thought that anyone who looked at them strangely was an enemy who wanted to hurt them, and sometimes they even got quite confused and tried to hurt their families.

The situation with the soldiers got them a lot of attention from doctors who found that they were suffering from something called Post Traumatic Stress Disorder (PTSD). With professional help, a lot of the soldiers were able to start to enjoy once more the lives that they had before the war.

In Iraq, the war had stopped but some of the local fighting kept going on. The insurgents still use car bombs to fight and some people are still scared of going to the market or out into the city. Large groups of Iraqi people don't have access to clean water or enough food, so a lot of kids and adults get sick pretty often.

Now, this is a good time to ask yourself a question: are things better or worse for the Iraqi people than they were before? In the past, the Iraqi people suffered from constant war and bad treatment from a mean leader. Since the 2003 Iraq War, have things gotten any better? Well, sadly, not much. The leaders are better in Iraq, but there is still lots of fighting and people still don't have enough food or water.

Worse yet, some of the reasons that were used to start the war turned out to be wrong. Do you remember the three main reasons that President Bush mentioned when he said that the United States was going to war? As we saw earlier, the United States and United Kingdom wanted to:

1. Take care of the whole Weapons of Mass Destruction (WMD) problem.
2. Replace Saddam Hussein as president, because he was such a cruel person.
3. Stop Iraq from supporting terrorist groups like Al-Qaeda.

Well, two of those reasons (the first one and the last one) ended up being wrong. There were no new WMDs ever found in Iraq, and there was no proof that Iraq was making any new ones or that they even had plans to do so. Also, there was never any connection found between the government of Iraq and

Al-Qaeda, the group that destroyed the Twin Towers on 9/11.

Looking back, some people feel that the Iraq War was a mistake. They feel that thousands of Americans, Britons, Iraqis, and others died for no reason. They feel that the people of the world were lied to in order to get them to support the war, and that the war itself was not handled well.

Why it is impossible for anyone to know everything at the beginning of a war, do you think that President Bush and Prime Minister Blair should have waited more time before invading Iraq or do you think that they made the right decision with the information that they had? Why not ask some adults that you know what they think about the war and why they have that opinion?

Conclusion

We have learned a lot about the Iraq War in this book. We saw how it began, what happened during it, and how it ended. Do you think that you could share with someone else all that you learned about the war? Let's review some of the most important points together.

In the first chapter, we saw how the Gulf War, fought in 1991, planted the seeds of the Iraq War. Specifically, the war that Saddam Hussein chose to deal with the international community caused serious problems and made other nations want to invade his country. Remember, Saddam Hussein had promised to let international inspectors into his country to look for Weapons of mass Destruction. But when he began to stop letting them in and to make it more difficult for them to do their jobs, the United Nations sent Resolution 1441 to try to force him. When things still moved slowly, the U.S. and U.K. didn't want to wait any longer and invaded Iraq on March 20, 2003.

Then we saw why the war happened. In his speech just before the Iraq War began, President George W. Bush explained the three main reasons for the bombing and invasion of Iraq. We looked at each of the reasons one by one, and you were able to decide for yourself whether or not you agreed with them and whether or not you thought it was a good idea to invade Iraq. Do you remember the three reasons? The

Coalition wanted to remove Saddam Hussein from power, wanted to get rid of the WMDs, and wanted to make sure that Iraq stopped supporting terrorist groups like Al-Qaeda. Those were the main reasons for the 2003 Iraq War.

Then we saw what happened during the war. We saw that the war was divided up into two phases: the initial combat phase (which only lasted from March 20 to May 1, 2003) and then the much longer rebuilding phase. The rebuilding phase is what was the most difficult. The fighting in Iraq seemed to go on and on, and as American soldiers kept dying in the fighting, people back home in the United States started to think that the war was not such a brilliant idea after all. They saw that the Iraq invasion had turned into a civil war, and that maybe America shouldn't be involved anymore. Also, we saw the power of the news media. We saw how several stories that came out in the news made some Americans think that the White House was not truly doing a good job in Iraq at all. We also saw that the use of private citizens to rebuild Iraq was unpopular with some Americans and even led to some problems in Iraq.

Then we saw what it was like to be a kid during the Iraq War. Whether you were a kid living in Iraq during the fighting or were back in the United States learning about it in school, you would have been sure to have had an opinion about all the fighting and violence. Also, people that you knew and loved would have been affected by the war, something decided by people in an office far away. Kids often have a hard time understanding wars, and the Iraq War was a confusing time for lots of people- adults included.

Then we learned about how the Iraq War ended. After a long time, the rebuilding phase finally came to a close, and the American troops left Iraq in December 0f 2011. Were they successful in their mission to leave Iraq a better place than they found it? What do you think? We were able to compare Iraq before and after the 2003 invasion, and to be honest, Iraq is still a pretty rough place to live in. The following chapter showed us what Iraq is like today and how most of the people view the 2003 Iraq War. Do you remember what many people think about the war? Many people, both American and Iraqi, think that the war was a lousy idea.

The Iraq War was a time when the United States continued its close relationship with Great Britain and chose to ignore what many other countries were saying. Instead of waiting for the United Nations to give them permission to act (like what had happened in 1991 before the Gulf War) the U.S. and the U.K. decided for themselves what the best course of action was and went ahead with it.

The international community wasn't happy with any part of the Iraq War. While some nations helped out in different ways, others decided not to be such close friends with the United States. In fact, for many people living around the world, the United States became less like a helpful friend and more like a big bully. To this day American politicians still talk about and argue about the Iraq War, and they can't agree on whether or not it was a good idea.

What about you? Well, while you may not be the President of the United States (yet!), do you think that there are any lessons for you to learn after reading this book? Of course there are. One of them has to do with getting all of the information before getting into a fight. Sometime you might hear a rumor and it may not be true at all. Before you get too angry, you should always make sure of the facts. President Bush and Primer Minister Blair didn't have all the facts when they invaded Iraq. If they had known what we know now, maybe things would have been different. So whenever someone tells you something that makes you angry, be sure to make sure that what they said was true.

Also, it is a good idea to learn something from President Obama. When he became president in 2009, the Iraq War had been going on for a long time. However, he knew when it was time to walk away from the fight. He knew that no matter how many more soldiers he sent to Iraq that things weren't going to change that way. You can learn the same lesson: learn when it is time to just walk away from something. Whether you are arguing, fighting, or being bullied, sometimes you know that nothing good will happen if you stick around. So be like President Obama and be smart enough to leave when it is time.

The 2003 Iraq War was a time when the news helped people to see what was happening on the other side of the world almost instantly. There were lots of opinions, and lots of people died- including President Saddam Hussein. What do you think: if you had been old enough, would you have fought in the Iraq War or would you have protested against it? Would you have tried to help the Iraqi people one way or another?

Iraqi boys flash peace signs[12]

---

[12] Image source: http://www.boman12.org/issues-peace.htm

Made in the USA
San Bernardino, CA
09 September 2015